THE NATURE KIDS GUIDE TO
SNOW LEOPARDS

DAVID ANDERSON

LP Media Inc. Publishing
Text copyright © 2026 by LP Media Inc.
All rights reserved.

For information address LP Media Inc. Publishing,
30012 Variolite St NW, Princeton MN 55371
www.lpmedia.org

Publication Data

Snow Leopards
The Nature Kid's Guide to Snow Leopards — First edition.

Summary: "Learn all about Snow Leopards, the Nature Kid Way"
— Provided by publisher.

ISBN: 979-8-89818-128-4

[1. Snow Leopards – Non-Fiction] I. Title.

Title: The Nature Kid's Guide to Snow Leopards

CONTENTS

MOUNTAIN GHOSTS

Snow leopards are sometimes called "ghosts of the mountains." People rarely see them in the wild. Their pale gray fur blends perfectly with rocky slopes.

Growl! A snow leopard climbs on a cold, rocky cliff.

Snow leopards live high in the mountains, where it is very cold and rocky. They usually live between 6,000 and 18,000 feet of **elevation** above the ground. Some snow leopards even live above the clouds.

They rest in caves and on rocky ledges. Their thick fur keeps them warm, and their wide paws help them walk on snow and ice.

Snow leopards travel far to find food. They can walk up to 27 miles in one night. These strong cats are made for life in the high mountains.

ASIAN ALPS

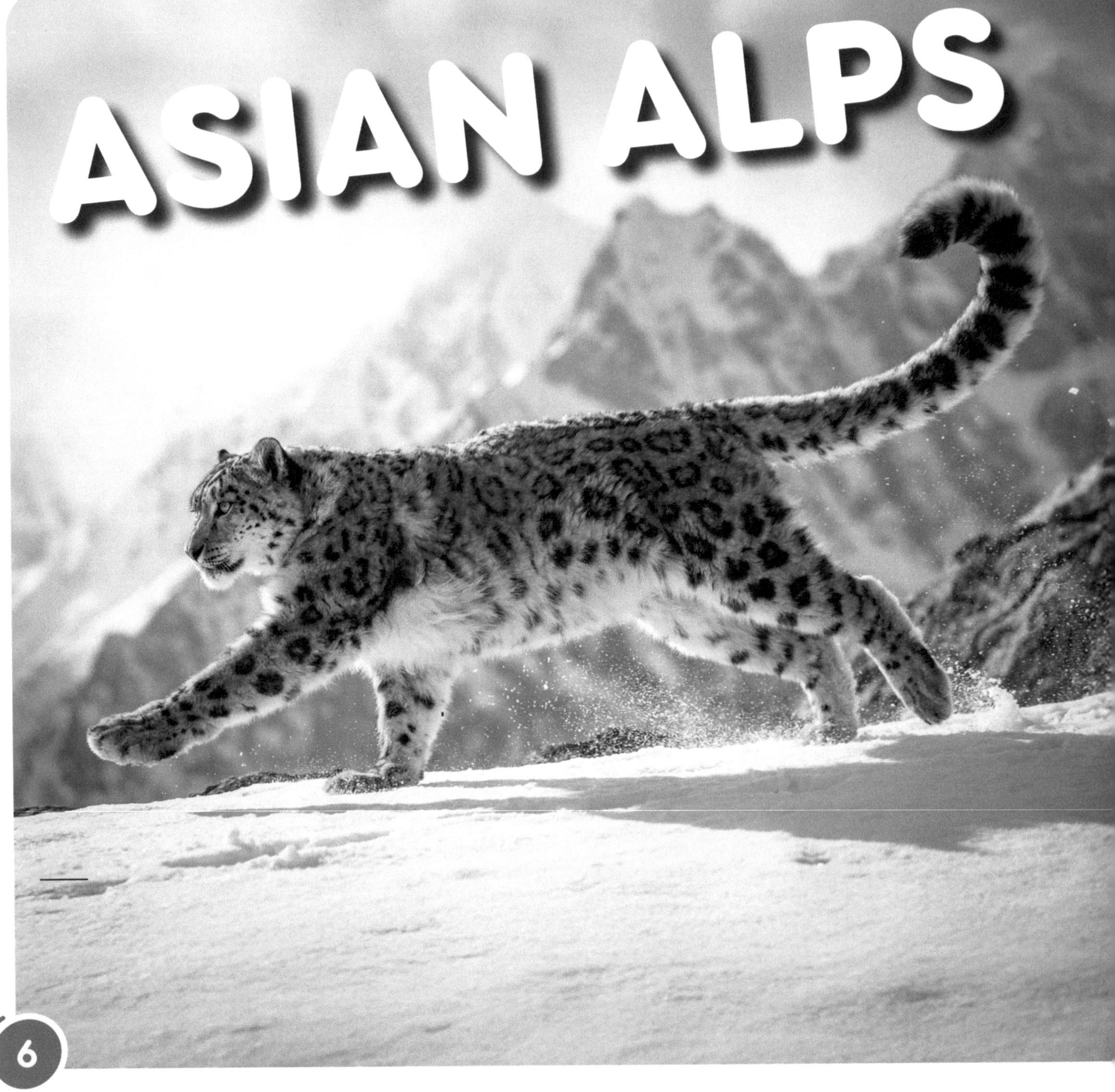

Whoosh! A snow leopard runs across a snowy ridge. Its tail floats behind.

Snow leopards live only in Asia. They roam across 12 countries. You can find them from Afghanistan to Mongolia.

These cats live in the Himalayas. They also live in the Altai and Tian Shan mountains. All of these are very high peaks.

Each cat needs a large area to hunt. Some have home ranges of 400 square miles. That is bigger than many cities!

China has the most snow leopards. About 60 percent of all snow leopards live there.

SIZE UP

Pounce! A snow leopard leaps between two rocks. It lands softly.

Snow leopards are medium-sized big cats. They are much smaller than lions and tigers, but closer to the size of a large dog.

They weigh between 60 and 120 pounds. Males are usually larger than females.

Their body is between 3 to 4 feet long. Their thick tails add another 3 feet.

Snow leopards stand about 2 feet tall at the shoulder. That is as tall as a German Shepherd.

BUILT TOUGH

Snow leopards have extra strong chest muscles. They help the cat breathe thin air.

Crunch! A snow leopard walks on icy ground. Its wide paws grip tight.

Snow leopards have thick fur all over their bodies. Their fur can be 5 inches long on their bellies. This keeps them warm in freezing weather.

These cats have wide, furry paws. Their paws work like snowshoes. They help the cat walk on deep snow without sinking.

Snow leopards have short, rounded ears. These small ears lose less heat than big ears would. Their large noses also help in the cold. They warm the air before it reaches the cat's lungs.

SUPER
SENSES

Snap! A snow leopard turns its head. It hears a sound far away.

Snow leopards have amazing eyesight. They can spot prey from over a mile away. Their pale green or gray eyes are built for hunting.

These cats see well in dim light. This helps them hunt at dawn and dusk. Their large eyes gather more light than human eyes.

Snow leopards watch for movement on rocky slopes.

SNEAKY
SPOTS

Snarl! A snow leopard hides among gray rocks. Can you spot it?

Snow leopards have spotted coats. Their fur is gray and white with dark spots. This pattern is called **camouflage**.

The spots help them hide on rocky mountains. Prey cannot see them against the stones. This makes hunting easier.

Each snow leopard has a unique spot pattern. This means no two cats look exactly the same. Scientists use these patterns to tell them apart.

Snow leopard spots are called rosettes. They look like little roses!

MEATY
MENU

Growl! A snow leopard guards it's food hidden on a rocky ledge.

Snow leopards are **carnivores**, which means they eat meat. Their favorite food is wild sheep and goats.

Blue sheep are a main food source, but snow leopards also hunt ibex. Ibex are wild goats with long, curved horns.

Snow leopards eat smaller animals too. They catch marmots, hares, and birds. One large meal can feed a cat for two weeks.

Snow leopards eat their prey over three or four days. The cold air keeps it fresh.

SNEAK ATTACK

Snow leopards often hunt at dawn or dusk when shadows help hide them from prey.

Shhhh! A snow leopard creeps low. Its belly brushes the snow.

Snow leopards are ambush hunters. They sneak up on prey before attacking. Their spotted coats help them stay hidden.

These cats are patient. A snow leopard may watch its prey for hours. It waits for the perfect moment to strike.

Snow leopards attack from above when they can. They leap down from rocks to surprise their prey. A snow leopard can jump up to 50 feet in one bound.

Once they catch prey, they drag it to a safe spot. There, they keep it hidden from other hunters.

WATCH OUT

Screech! A golden eagle soars above the peaks.

Adult snow leopards are **apex predators**. This means they are at the top of the food chain. Almost nothing hunts them.

But young cubs face danger. Golden eagles may attack them from above. Wolves sometimes come into their area too.

Humans are the only danger to adult Snow Leopards. It is against the law the hunt them, but some people still do. It is called poaching.

Only about 4,000 to 6,500 snow leopards are left in the wild today.

STAY SAFE

Rumble! Rocks tumble down a steep slope. A snow leopard dashes away.

Snow leopards have many ways to stay safe. Their gray and white fur blends into rocky slopes. This makes them hard to see.

These cats know their **territory** well. They use hidden caves and rocky dens to rest safely.

Snow leopards stay alert. If something seems wrong, they slip away quietly on fur-covered paws.

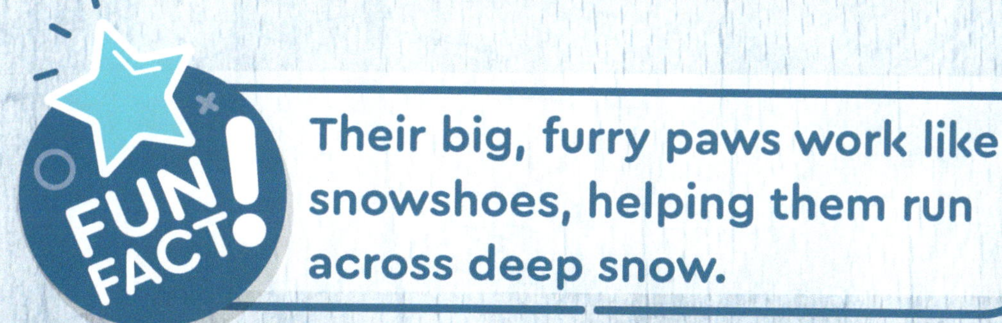

LEAP LORDS

Thump! A snow leopard lands on a rocky ledge.

Snow leopards are amazing jumpers. Their back legs are very strong. This helps them leap across wide gaps between rocks.

Their long tails help them balance. A snow leopard's tail can be three feet long. It helps them balance even on small ledges.

These cats move easily on steep cliffs. They climb up or down slopes no other animals can climb.

Snow leopards can leap six times their body length in a single jump. That is about 50 feet!

DAWN PATROL

Hiss! A snow leopard stretches in the dim light. It is time to hunt.

Snow leopards are most active at dawn and dusk. This time is called twilight. The low light helps them hunt without being seen.

During the day, snow leopards rest on cliffs or ridges. They watch their surroundings and save energy for hunting.

At night, they may travel many miles. They walk along the same paths to patrol their home range.

Snow leopards have been seen traveling across deserts and open land to patrol their territory and find food.

LONE ROAMERS

Rustle! A snow leopard walks alone through mountain grass.

Snow leopards live alone most of the time. Each cat has its own territory, which is the area it lives and hunts in. They do not share this space with other snow leopards.

These cats mark their territory with scent. This tells other snow leopards to stay away and look for another place to live.

The only time snow leopards stay together is when a mother is raising her cubs.

A snow leopard's territory can cover up to 400 square miles of mountain land.

29

FINDING LOVE

Male snow leopards will follow a female for days. They wait until she is ready to mate.

Howl! A snow leopard calls out. Who is listening?

Snow leopards live alone most of the time. But once a year, they meet up to mate. This happens in late winter.

Their scent marks on rocks and plants tell other snow leopards they are nearby.

The females also make loud calling sounds to let males know they are ready to mate. The males follow these sounds and scent trails to find them.

The cats stay together for a few days. Then they go back to living alone. Cubs are born between April and July.

CUDDLY CUBS

Squeak! Tiny cubs cuddle close to their mother for warmth.

Snow leopard cubs weigh about one pound at birth. They are very small and helpless. A mother usually has two or three cubs at once.

Cubs are born with their eyes closed, but they open them after about one week. Their fur is also darker than adult fur at this age.

Cubs stay in a rocky den for the first few months. This keeps them safe and warm. They drink milk for about two months before they start eating meat.

Snow leopard mothers purr to their cubs. Adults cannot roar like lions. They chuff to say hello!

MOM KNOWS

Snort! A mother snow leopard watches her cubs play nearby.

Mother snow leopards raise cubs alone. They do all the work, with no help from the father.

Mothers teach cubs how to hunt. Cubs watch their mother stalk prey. Then they practice what they learned on small animals like marmots.

Cubs stay with their mother for about 18 to 22 months. During this time, they learn everything they need to survive. Then they leave to find their own territory.

Mothers move cubs to new dens often to keep them safe from predators.

TROUBLE
AHEAD

Crack! A fence post breaks. A snow leopard slips through.

Snow leopards face many dangers today. Scientists think only 4,000 to 6,500 remain in the wild.

Farmers sometimes harm snow leopards. The cats may hunt sheep or goats when wild prey is hard to find.

Climate change is also a problem. Warmer weather pushes animals higher up mountains, shrinking their habitat.

Poachers hunt snow leopards for their fur. One coat can sell for over $5,000 on the black market.

HELPING HANDS

Click! A snow leopard walks past a camera. Scientists are taking pictures to help save them.

Many people work to save snow leopards. Scientists put special collars on some cats. The collars track where the leopards go.

Local people help too. Some farmers get paid to keep snow leopards safe on their land.

Zoos around the world also help. They raise snow leopards to increase the population. They teach people about them.

Twelve countries work together. They protect snow leopards and their mountain homes.

GLOSSARY

elevation
How high up a place is from the ground below.

camouflage
Colors or patterns that help an animal hide by blending in.

carnivores
Animals that eat only meat.

apex predators
Animals at the top that no other animals hunt.

territory
The area where an animal lives and calls its own.

www.ingramcontent.com/pod-product-compliance
Lightning Source LLC
Chambersburg PA
CBHW041620110726
48005CB00002B/456